THIS COOKBOOK

BELONGS TO:

____

O. Halverson & Co.
PUBLISHING
U.S.A.

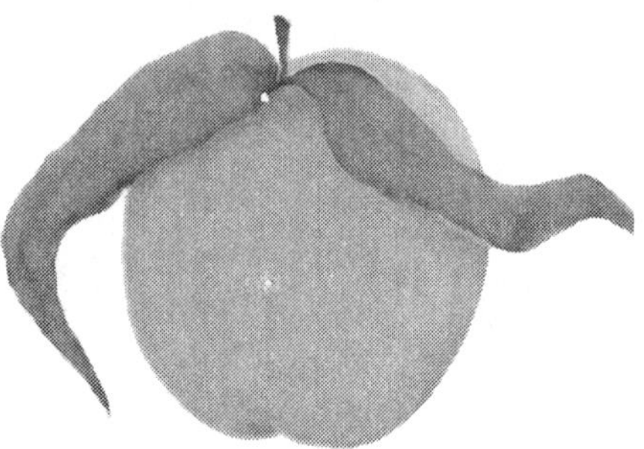

Published by
O. Halverson & Co. Publishing
P.O. Box 827
Brigham City, Utah 84302

Orders: 1.435.723.6611
www.brighamdistributing.com

ISBN: 0-9785812-0-2
Copyright ©2006 O. Halverson & Co. Publishing

Printed in United States of America

Cover Art ©2006 Lori Nawyn **www.lorinawyn.com**
Graphic Design ©2006 Lori Nawyn **www.lorinawyn.com**

Peach 101: Recipes Your Mother Never Told You About
http://Peach101.blogspot.com

To my husband and children,
for cheering me on.

To my friend, Phyllis Valentine,
who taught me that cooking with
peaches is as wonderful as
eating them right off the tree.

To my neighbors and family,
who taste-tested and shared recipes.

Special thanks to Michael Bezas
and his wonderful wife, Cindy.
And thanks, as always,
to my friend, Janie.

Peach 101: Recipes Your Mother Never Told You About
is a mix of several never before published recipes with a few
old favorites sprinkled in to round things out!

TABLE OF CONTENTS

Tips on Using Peaches 9

Appetizers & Beverages

Hot Buttered Peach Juice 12 - Peachy Lemonade 13 - Best in the West Peach Shake 14 - Peach Blueberry Smoothie 15 - Peach Nog 16 - Peach Cocoa 17 - Fruit Slush 18

Soups and Salads

Turkey Spinach Salad 20 - Peach Poppy Seed Vinaigrette 21 - Bezas' Peach and Feta Summer Salad 22 - Creamy Peach Soup 23 - Yummy Fruit Salad 24 - Three Layer Tropical Summer Salad 25 - Peach Fluff 'n Stuff 26 - Michael's Garbanzo Peach Soup 27 - Peach Royalle 28

Main Dishes & Side Dishes

Grilled Turkey Cutlets 30 - Grilled Shrimp and Peaches 31 - Ham Stuffed Peaches 32 - Grilled Sausage and Peach Skewers 33 - Sharon's Glazed Peaches and Pork 34 - Southwestern Peach Divan 35 - Tropical Baby Carrots 36 - Sweet Mashed Sweet Potatoes 37 - Peaches 'n Beans 38 - Peach Glazed Carrots 39 - Asparagus with Mock Hollandaise 40 - Baked Peach 41 - Fresh Fruit Kabobs 42 - Cheesy Peaches 43

Breads & Muffins

Oatmeal Peachies 46 - Peach Zucchini Bread 47 - Easy Cran-Peach Corn Bread Muffins 48 - Oatmeal Peach Bread 49 - Old Fashioned Peach Bread 50

Pies & Cakes

Peach of a Pecan Pie 52 - Brigham City Peach Jumble Pie 53 - Peaches and Cream Pie 54 - Baby Pies 55 - Fran's Peach Pie 56 - Grandmother's Special White Cake 57 - Peach Cake 58 - Gingerbread Peach Cake 59 - Cream Cheese Peach Cake 60

Cookies & Cobblers

Individual Peachie Pizzas 62 - Peach Dainties 63 - Peach Coconut Chews 64 - Peach Snickerdoodles 65 - Esther's Cobbler 66 - Caramel Cobbler 67 - Fast Peach Cobbler 68 - Jammin' Spiced Peach Cookies 69

Desserts

Tangy Peach Pudding 72 - Old Fashioned Peach Pudding 73 - Peaches n' Chips 74 - Peach Sorbet 75 - Peach Squares 76 - Raspberry Peach Supreme 77 - Peach Shorties 78 - Easy Melba 79 - Peach Tapioca 80 - Harvest Trifle 81 - Stuffed Fresh Peaches 82 - Cheesecake with Peach Glaze 83 - Peach Banana Sherbet 84 - Jello Melba 85 - Baked Peach/Rice Pudding 86 - Peach Bars 87 - Peach Bread Pudding 88 - Quick Peach Ice Cream 89 - Peach Supreme Ice Cream 90

Breakfasts

Peach Fritters 92 - Whole Wheat Waffles with Peach Syrup 93 - Fruity Hash Browns 94 - Hearty Peach Flapjacks 95 - Oatmeal Mix 96 - Breakfast Cobbler 97 - Peach Granola 98 - Peach Crepes 99 - Susan's Hot Peach Breakfast 100 - Sausage Peach Scramble 101 - Peach Roll-ups 102 - Peachy Keen French Toast 103 - Grandma's Peach Cinnamon Rolls 104

This 'n That

Sweet Fruit Salsa 106 - Peach Salsa 107 - Cranberry Peach Relish 108 - Peach Popsicles 109 - Peach Leather 110 - Peach Spread 111 - Peach Jam 112 - Peach Facial Scrub and Peach Face Mask 113 - Sour Cream Topping 114 - Can't Get Enough Peach Popcorn Bake 115 - Spiced Peach Refrigerator Jam 116 - Peach Honey Butter 117 - Peachy Angel Frosting 118 - Tropical Ham Sauce 119 - Peach Honey Frosting 120 - Peach Glaze 121 - Popcorn Balls 122

Tips on Using Peaches

1. There are many varieties of peaches which are frequently sold according to the color of their flesh: white, yellow or red. White and yellow peaches have a similar flavor but white peaches are generally sweeter and less acidic. Red fleshed peaches bear a flavor that is more tart. Peaches are categorized as clingstone, freestone, or semi-freestone. In clingstones, the flesh of the peach "clings" to the stone, or pit. In freestones, the peach flesh pulls easily away from the stone. Semi-free-stones, a hybrid of the clingstone and freestone, are smaller in size and have a stone that detaches easily when the fruit is fully ripened. Freestones are the most popular peaches for baking, canning, and freezing.

2. Select peaches that have a "peachy" fragrance and that give slightly to gentle pressure. A rosy "blush" is not always a good indicator of ripeness and varies from one variety to another. Look for peaches with velvety skins and creamy yellow or golden undertones. Avoid peaches with blemishes, bruising or a greenish hue and those that feel very hard.

3. Three to four medium peaches equal 1 pound, 1 pound equals 2 cups of sliced peaches or 1 cup puree. A bushel of peaches will yield approximately 18-24 quarts of peaches for canning.

4. Because peaches spoil quickly, it's best to purchase only the quantity that you plan to use in a short time. To help keep ripe peaches fresh refrigerate them for up to 3-5 days. The longer peaches are refrigerated, however, the more the juice and flavor will lessen. To bring out the full flavor of the fruit, peaches should be removed from refrigeration 30 minutes prior to consumption.

Firm/unripe peaches should not be stored in the refrigerator as the cold will prevent them from ripening and destroy the flavor.

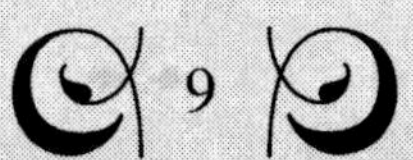

Instead, store unripe peaches at room temperature, out of direct sunlight. Ripening can be hastened by placing peaches in a paper bag with an apple, or banana, at room temperature. Loosely close the top of the bag to allow "breathing room." Peaches are ready to eat when they're barely soft, usually within two or three days. Never store fresh peaches in plastic bags as this will change their flavor and texture.

5. To preserve the integrity of the fruit, wash peaches in cool water only immediately before serving.

6. Peach skins can be removed with a paring knife but this tends to waste much of the flesh. Another method is to dip peaches in boiling water for 30-60 seconds until the skins loosen. Then, quickly plunge the fruit into ice cold water. When cool enough to handle, they will be easy to peel with a sharp paring knife. Start at the top of the peach and pull the skin downward.

Yet another alternative is to microwave the peach at full power for 15 seconds. Allow the fruit to stand for 2 minutes before attempting to remove the skin.

7. To remove pits, use a small knife and start cutting at the stem. Follow the natural indentation and cut the peach down to the pit around the entire perimeter. Twist the halves apart. Remove pit with the knife or with your fingers.

8. To prevent browning and help retain the fresh, bright appearance of the fruit, dip fresh cut peaches into a mixture of 1 cup water and 1 tablespoon lemon juice. You can also try sprinkling them with orange juice or toss sliced peaches with thawed orange juice concentrate.

9. For long-term storage, peaches can be frozen, canned, or dried. For more information consult your local extension office, fruit growers association or the Internet.

Appetizers & Beverages

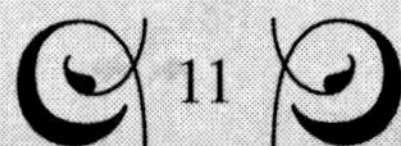

Hot Buttered Peach Juice

3/4 cup peach juice
1/2 cup lemon juice
3/4 cup sugar
1 teaspoon instant lemon peel
4 cups water
6 teaspoons butter
6 cinnamon sticks

In medium saucepan, combine juices, sugar, peel, and water. Bring to a boil then reduce heat and simmer for 3 minutes, stirring occasionally. Pour into cups. Top each with a teaspoon of butter and stir with cinnamon sticks.

Peachy Lemonade

Peach sorbet (see recipe on page 75)
1 can frozen lemonade concentrate
Water

Pour sorbet mixture into ice cube trays and freeze.
Mix frozen lemonade and specified amount of water
according to directions on can. Pour lemonade into
glasses and add peach cubes.

Best in the West Peach Milk Shake

6 fresh or canned peaches
5 cups peach ice cream
3/4 cup cream soda
1 teaspoon vanilla
1/2 teaspoon lemon extract
Ground pecans

In blender, puree peaches. Add three scoops ice cream and blend. Add remaining ice cream, cream soda, vanilla and lemon extract and blend until smooth. Top with pecans and serve immediately!

Peach Blueberry Smoothie

Peach sorbet (see recipe on page 75)
2 cups yogurt
Frozen blueberries

Pour sorbet mixture into ice cube trays and freeze.
Put yogurt into blender. Remove frozen peach cubes
from trays and add desired amount of cubes to yogurt.
Blend until smooth. Add desired amount of blueberries
to yogurt mixture and again blend until smooth.

Peach Nog

1 quart eggnog
1 quart peach juice
2 cans (29 ounces each) peaches, pureed
1 teaspoon vanilla
Nutmeg

In punch bowl, combine eggnog, peach juice, peach puree, and vanilla. Stir well and chill. When ready to serve, sprinkle with nutmeg.

*If desired, float scoops of eggnog flavored ice cream in punch bowl or put 1 scoop of eggnog flavored ice cream in each cup of Peach Nog.

Peach Cocoa
with
whipped Marshmallow Creme

2 tablespoons peach juice
1 tablespoon peach flavored Jello
1 cup marshmallow creme
1/3 cup whipped topping, thawed
3 cups water
1 cup peach juice
4-5 scoops instant milk chocolate cocoa mix (to taste)
1/4 cup French vanilla creamer
1/4 teaspoon almond extract (optional)
Nutmeg (optional)

In small microwave safe bowl, heat peach juice on high for 30 seconds. Add Jello and stir until dissolved. Combine marshmallow creme with warm Jello mixture. Add whipped topping and whip until smooth. Place in freezer until set.

Meanwhile, in medium saucepan, bring water and juice to a boil. Add cocoa mix, creamer, and extract (if desired), and stir until smooth. Pour into four cups. Remove marshmallow creme mixture from freezer and add a dollop to each cup of cocoa. If desired, sprinkle with nutmeg. Serve immediately.

Fruit Slush

1 cup sugar
1/2 cup pineapple or peach juice
1 can (12 ounces) orange juice, thawed
1 can (15 ounces) diced peaches
1 can (20 ounces) crushed pineapple
1 package (16 ounces) frozen raspberries
2 cups Ginger Ale
Ginger Ale

In small saucepan, stir sugar and pineapple or peach juice until sugar is dissolved. Bring mixture to a boil. Remove from heat. In large, freezer safe container or 2 quart baking dish combine sugar/juice mixture, orange juice, peaches, pineapple, raspberries, and Ginger Ale. Mix well. Cover and freeze overnight. When ready to serve, remove from freezer and allow to stand at room temperature for 20-30 minutes. Scoop into glasses then fill with Ginger Ale.

Soups & Salads

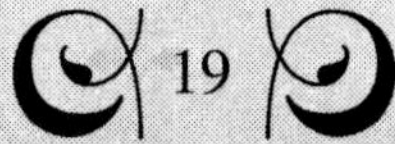

Turkey Spinach Salad

7 cups fresh baby spinach
1/2 cup toasted sliced almonds
3/4 cup cooked chicken or turkey, cut into thin strips
2 cups fresh ripe peaches, cut into bite sized pieces
Peach Poppy seed Vinaigrette (See page 21 for recipe)

Toss spinach and almonds. Place on plates and top with chicken (or turkey) strips and peaches. Drizzle with Peach Poppy seed Vinaigrette (see recipe on page 21).

Peach Poppy Seed Vinaigrette

1/3 cup peach jam
1/3 cup white wine vinegar
1/4 cup olive oil
1 tablespoon honey, warmed
1 teaspoon poppy seeds

Combine all ingredients in a jar. Chill, shake well, serve.

Bezas' Peach and Feta Summer Salad

1 tablespoon balsamic vinegar
2 teaspoons fresh lemon juice
2 teaspoons honey
1/4 teaspoon salt
3 tablespoons cold-pressed extra virgin olive oil

4 fresh ripe peaches
1 small head butter lettuce
2 cups fresh baby spinach leaves
2 cups red romaine
1/2 cup crumbled feta cheese
1/4 cup chopped walnuts
1/4 cup pine nuts
Cracked pepper (to taste)
Dill weed (to taste)

Create the dressing by mixing together vinegar, lemon juice, honey, and salt; stir well. Add the oil and blend well. Peel and slice the peaches. Tear the greens into bite-sized pieces then toss and place on individual salad plates. Distribute the peaches, feta, and nuts evenly on top of the salad greens. Drizzle the dressing over each serving.

*Optional: add cracked pepper and/or sprinkle lightly with dill weed.

Creamy Peach Soup

3/4 cup sour cream (or yogurt)
1 cup peach syrup (see recipe on page 93)
1/2 cup peach juice
Fresh or canned peaches, thinly sliced
Nutmeg or cloves (optional)

Whisk together sour cream (or yogurt), peach syrup, and peach juice. Chill for several hours before serving. Garnish with peach slices. If desired, sprinkle with nutmeg or cloves.

Yummy Fruit Salad

1 package (6 ounces) peach Jello
1-1/2 cups boiling water
1 package (3 ounces) cream cheese
1 cup diced canned peaches
1 banana, sliced
1 cup crushed pineapple
1 cup Mandarin orange slices
1/2 cup pecans
1 cup whipped cream

Dissolve peach Jello in boiling water. Gradually add cream cheese and blend until smooth. Chill until slightly thickened. Fold in peaches, banana, pineapple, orange slices, and pecans. Beat whipped cream until stiff then add to Jello mixture. Pour into 1 and 1/4 quart mold. Chill until set.

Three Layer Tropical Summer Salad

1 package (3 ounces) lemon Jello
1 cup boiling water
1 cup Sprite
2 cups small curd cottage cheese

1 package (3 ounces) peach Jello
1 cup boiling water
1 cup pineapple juice (reserved from pineapple pieces)
1 cup diced canned peaches
1 cup canned pineapple tidbits

1 package (3 ounces) pineapple Jello
1 cup boiling water
1 cup Sprite
1/2 package mini-marshmallows

Dissolve lemon Jello in 1 cup boiling water. Add 1 cup Sprite. Cool slightly. Fold in cottage cheese. Pour into 13x9 pan and chill until set. Dissolve peach Jello in 1 cup boiling water. Add pineapple juice, peaches, and pineapple tidbits. Chill until set. Dissolve pineapple Jello in 1 cup boiling water. Add 1 cup Sprite. Pour on top of other layers. Top with marshmallows and chill until firmly set.

Peach Fluff 'n Stuff

3 cups cold water
1 package (3 ounces) cook and serve tapioca pudding
1 package (3 ounces) cook and serve vanilla pudding
1 package (3 ounces) peach flavored Jello
1 carton (8 ounces) Cool Whip
1 can (15 ounces) diced peaches, drained

Put water in medium saucepan. Stir in tapioca pudding, vanilla pudding, and Jello. Bring mixture to a
boil, stirring constantly. Remove from heat. Allow
to cool slightly then fold in Cool Whip and peaches.
Chill until set.

Michael's Garbanzo Peach Soup

1 can (15 ounces) garbanzo beans, drained
1/4 - 1/2 cup milk (depending on desired thickness)
3 or 4 fresh ripe peaches, peeled and diced
1/4 teaspoon cinnamon
1-1/2 tablespoon lemon juice
1/4 teaspoon ginger
2 tablespoon sugar

Blend garbanzo beans and milk until pureed. Add peaches and blend well. While blending, add cinnamon, lemon juice, ginger, and sugar. Blend for two minutes. Chill overnight. Serve in a bowl with a mint sprig placed in the middle.

Peach Royalle

1 pre made graham cracker pie crust
1 package (6 ounces) raspberry Jello
1/2 cup boiling water
4 ounces cream cheese, softened
1 cup fresh, canned, or frozen (thawed) peaches
1 cup frozen blueberries, thawed
Whipped cream
Fresh blueberries
Fresh peaches

In medium pan, dissolve Jello in boiling water. Remove from heat and stir in cream cheese. Whisk until smooth. Pour into medium sized bowl. Chill until partially set. Fold in peaches and blueberries. Pour onto crust. Chill until firm. Top with whipped cream and garnish with fresh peaches and blueberries.

Main Dishes & Side Dishes

Grilled Turkey Cutlets

3/4 cup peach preserves
1/2 cup barbecue sauce
6 turkey cutlets

In large bowl, stir together preserves and sauce. Pierce cutlets several times with a fork or sharp knife. Add cutlets and marinate overnight. Remove cutlets and place on medium grill. Cook through (approximately 6 - 8 minutes) basting with remaining sauce.

*Tastes great on chicken too!

Grilled Shrimp and Peaches with Coconut Sauce

1 cup brown sugar
1/4 cup peach juice
1/4 cup butter
1/3 cup almond milk
1/3 cup honey
1 fresh ripe peach
1 ripe banana
1 cup shredded coconut
3-4 pounds shrimp
2-3 large fresh ripe peaches, sliced

In small sauce pan combine brown sugar, peach juice, and butter. Stir over medium heat until butter is melted and brown sugar is dissolved. Remove from heat. In blender combine almond milk, honey, peach, and banana. Blend until smooth.

In large bowl, combine brown sugar mixture and mixture from blender. Stir until well blended. Fold in coconut. Add shrimp and peaches and coat well. Grill over medium heat until shrimp is cooked through.

Ham Stuffed Peaches

2 ham slices, finely chopped
2 green onions, thinly sliced
2 ounces cream cheese
Salt and pepper to taste
1 can (29 ounces) peach halves, drained
Buttered bread crumbs

Preheat oven to 350.

Combine ham, onions, cream cheese, salt and pepper. Place peach halves in shallow baking dish. Fill centers of peaches with scoop of ham mixture and top with bread crumbs. Bake at 350 degrees for 15 minutes.

Grilled Sausage and Peach Skewers
with Zippy Peach marinade

1 red onion, cut into 1/2 inch chunks
1 package turkey sausage, cut sausages into 1/2 inch slices
1 zucchini, sliced to 1/2 inch thickness
2 fresh ripe peaches, cut into 1/2 inch chunks

On wooden skewers, alternate onion chunks with sau
sage, zucchini, and peaches. Cook on medium hot grill
and baste with marinade.

Marinade:

1/2 cup peach syrup (see recipe on page 93)
1/4 cup lemon juice
1 tablespoon white wine vinegar
1 tablespoon melted butter
1 tablespoon Heinz 57 sauce
1/8 teaspoon Worchestershire Sauce

Stir all ingredients together and brush onto skewers

* Also great on beef, turkey, or chicken!

Sharon's Glazed Peaches and Pork

1 jar (18 ounces) peach jam or preserves
1 bottle (8 ounces) Russian dressing
1 package dry Lipton Onion Soup mix
Pork loin pieces
1 can (29 ounces) sliced peaches, well drained

Stir together jam, dressing, and soup mix. Pour over
pork loin pieces and peaches in crock pot. Cook on
medium heat 4-5 hours; stir at least every 1/2 hour.

*Great served on a bed of rice!

Southwestern Peach Divan

2 packages (16 ounces each) frozen broccoli, cooked
2 cups cooked turkey, diced
2 cups peach slices, drained
1 can (4 ounces) green chilies
1/2 cup slivered almonds
1 can (10-3/4 ounces) Creamy Chicken Verde soup
1/2 cup milk
1/2 cup Miracle Whip
1/2 tablespoon lemon juice
1/4 teaspoon curry
1/2 cup snack cracker crumbs
2 teaspoons butter, melted

Preheat oven to 350.

Place cooked broccoli in bottom of 9x13 inch pan. Layer turkey, peaches, chilies, and almonds. In bowl, combine remaining ingredients and whisk until smooth. Pour over top of almonds. Combine crumbs and butter and crumble on top of soup mixture. Bake at 350 degrees until heated through, approximately 30 minutes.

Tropical Baby Carrots

1 package baby carrots
1 cup Old Fashioned Peach Pudding (see recipe page 73)
1/3 cup shredded coconut
1 tablespoon butter, melted

Preheat oven to 350.

Cook carrots until nearly tender. Drain and put into casserole dish. Stir together pudding, coconut, and butter. Pour over carrots. Bake at 350 for 10 minutes or until heated through.

Sweet Mashed Sweet Potatoes

6 large sweet potatoes
1/4 cup non-fat Half and Half
1/4 cup butter
3 tablespoons peach preserves

Preheat over to 350.

Wash and peel sweet potatoes. Wrap in foil and bake at 350 degrees until tender, approximately 1 hour. Carefully cube hot potatoes and place in large bowl. Add Half and Half, butter, and preserves. Mash or whip until smooth.

Peaches 'n Beans

1 can (15 ounces) sliced peaches, drained
2 tablespoons reserved syrup from peaches
2 tablespoons brown sugar
Cinnamon
1 can (16 ounces) Pork and Beans

In medium skillet, stir together syrup and sugar over medium heat. When sugar is dissolved, add peach slices and simmer. Sprinkle with cinnamon then stir in beans and heat through.

Peach Glazed Carrots

Preheat oven to 350.

1 small package baby carrots
3/4 cup water
1/3 cup brown sugar
2 teaspoons cornstarch
1/3 cup fresh or canned peaches, pureed

Preheat oven to 350 degrees.

Cook carrots until nearly tender. In small saucepan, combine water, brown sugar and cornstarch. Stirring constantly, cook over medium low heat until thickened. Stir in peaches. Arrange carrots in baking dish. Pour peach mixture over carrots and bake at 350 degrees for 10 minutes or until heated through.

Variation:

2 tablespoons butter
1/2 cup honey
1 tablespoon lemon juice
1/2 cup pureed peaches

Melt butter in saucepan. Add honey, lemon juice, and peaches. Add carrots and coat evenly. Bake for 8 minutes at 350 degrees.

Asparagus with Mock Hollandaise

1 pound asparagus, washed and par cooked

Sauce:

1/2 cup pureed fresh peach (slightly under ripe)
2 teaspoons butter, melted
1 tablespoon sour cream
1/2 teaspoon white wine vinegar
1/4 teaspoon cayenne pepper

Combine all ingredients in microwave safe bowl. Blend well. Microwave on high until heated through (30-40 seconds). Stir and pour over hot asparagus or chill and pour over cold asparagus.

*Also great on turkey!

Baked Peach

1 fresh ripe peach
2 teaspoons lemon juice
1/8 cup honey

Preheat oven to 350.

Wash and peel peach. Cut in half. Place halves in small casserole dish and prick with fork. Mix lemon juice and honey together and pour over peach halves. Cover and bake at 350 for 30 minutes, or until tender. Serve warm or cold.

Fresh Fruit Kabobs
with
Maraschino Orange Sauce

Fresh peaches
Strawberries
Kiwis
Wooden skewers

Prepare peaches by washing, peeling, and cutting into bite sized pieces. Wash strawberries and use either halves or whole. Wash, peel, and slice kiwis. Cut slices into halves. Alternate fruits on skewers. Place on platter or in rectangular container and drizzle with Maraschino orange sauce.

Maraschino orange sauce:

8 Maraschino cherries
6 ounces frozen orange juice, thawed
3 tablespoons juice from Maraschino cherries
1/4 cup peach juice
3 teaspoons sugar
1 tablespoon white wine vinegar

Puree cherries in blender or food processor. In small bowl, combine cherry puree, orange juice, cherry juice, peach juice, sugar, and vinegar. Blend well. Chill until ready to use.

Cheesy Peaches

1/2 cup cottage cheese
2 teaspoons honey
6 fresh or canned peach halves
Cinnamon

Preheat oven to 350 degrees.

Combine cottage cheese and honey. Spoon into peach halves. Sprinkle with cinnamon. Chill well and serve cold or bake at 350 for 15 minutes.

NOTES

One medium peach provides about 10 percent of the daily requirement of vitamin A and vitamin C.

Breads & Muffins

Oatmeal Peachies

1 box (7 ounces) Jiffy Oatmeal Muffin Mix
1/3 cup pureed fresh or frozen peaches
1 egg
1/4 cup chopped pecans

Prepare muffin mix according to package directions
except substitute peach puree for milk. Fold in pecans.
Bake according to package directions.

Peach Zucchini Bread

1 cup oil
2 cups sugar
3 eggs
1 cup shredded zucchini
1 cup fresh or canned peaches, diced
3 cups flour
1 teaspoon baking soda
1 teaspoon baking powder

Preheat oven to 325.

Beat oil, sugar, and eggs together. Stir in zucchini and peaches and mix well. Slowly stir in dry ingredients. Bake at 325 degrees for 60 minutes or until toothpick inserted in center of loaves comes out clean.

Easy Cran-Peach Corn Bread Muffins

1 box (8.5 ounces) Jiffy corn bread mix
1 egg, beaten
1/3 cup vanilla yogurt
1/4 cup fresh or canned peaches, chopped
1/4 cup cherry Craisins or dried cranberries

Mix together cornbread mix, egg, and yogurt (substitute yogurt for 1/3 cup milk on package directions). Fold in peaches and Craisins or cranberries. Bake according to package directions. Makes 6-8 muffins.

Oatmeal Peach Bread

2 eggs
1/3 cup oil
1/2 cup brown sugar
1 cup fresh or canned peaches, pureed
1 1/2 cups flour
1 teaspoon baking soda
1 teaspoon baking powder
1 teaspoon cinnamon
1/2 teaspoon nutmeg
1 cup quick oats
1/2 cup walnuts (optional)

Preheat oven to 350.

Beat together eggs, oil, and sugar. Add peaches and mix well. Combine dry ingredients and add to peach mixture. Stir until well blended. Pour into large greased loaf pan. Bake 50 minutes at 350 or until center is done.

Old Fashioned Peach Bread

1 cup sugar
3 cups butter
3 eggs
3 tablespoons sour cream
1 cup diced fresh peaches
1 teaspoon soda
1 teaspoon allspice
1 teaspoon cinnamon
1 teaspoon nutmeg
1 teaspoon ground cloves
2 cups flour
1 cup nuts

Preheat oven to 350.

Cream sugar, butter, and eggs. Add sour cream and peaches. Then add soda, spices, flour, and nuts. Bake in loaf pan at 350 degrees until center is firm.

Pies & Cakes

Peach of a Pecan Pie!

1 package (3 ounces) instant vanilla pudding
1 cup dark corn syrup
3/4 cup sweetened condensed milk
1/2 cup peach preserves
4 eggs, beaten
1-1/2 cups chopped pecans
2 8-inch pie shells, unbaked
Whipped cream, or vanilla ice cream
Fresh ripe peaches

Preheat oven to 375.

Blend pudding with corn syrup. Gradually stir in milk, preserves, and eggs. Add pecans. Pour into pie shells and bake at 375 until top is firm, about 40 minutes. Cool 4 hours or longer. Garnish with whipped cream, or vanilla ice cream, and peaches.

Brigham City Peach Jumble Pie

A delicious favorite!

2 cups fresh sliced rhubarb
1 1/3 cups sugar
1 cup water
1 package (3 ounces) strawberry kiwi flavored gelatin
2 cups canned peaches, cut into bite sized pieces
2 cups fresh strawberries, sliced into quarters

Place rhubarb in medium sauce pan with sugar and water. Stir until sugar is dissolved and bring to a boil over medium heat. Reduce heat. Stew rhubarb until just tender, about 3 to 5 minutes. Stir in gelatin until dissolved. Remove from heat. Allow to cool slightly before adding peaches and strawberries. Pour mixture into two 9 inch pie plates. Chill overnight, or until firmly set.

Topping:

1 cup peach juice
2 tablespoons flour
1/4 cup powdered sugar
1/3 cup granulated sugar
1 egg, well beaten
1/2 pint whipping cream
Wheat germ

Over medium heat, stir together juice, flour, sugars, and egg until smooth. Stirring constantly, bring to a boil. Boil one minute or until thickened. Remove and cool thoroughly. Whip cream. Fold into cooled mixture. Divide and spread over both pies. Sprinkle each pie with 1 tablespoon wheat germ.

Peaches and Cream Pie

1 9" pie shell
6 fresh ripe peaches, quartered
1 cup cream
2 eggs, beaten
1-1/2 teaspoon vanilla
1/4 cup sugar
2 tablespoons butter

Preheat oven to 350.

Arrange peach quarters in pie shell. Combine cream, eggs, vanilla, and sugar. Beat 3-5 minutes. Pour on top of peaches. Dot butter on top of cream by teaspoonfuls. Bake at 350 degrees for 1 hour or until filling is set and crust is browned.

Baby Pies

6 pre made miniature graham cracker crusts
1 package (3 ounces) vanilla pudding
Fresh peaches

Prepare pudding according to package directions.
Divide between crusts. Top with fresh peach slices.

Fran's Peach Pie

1-1/2 cups sugar
1/3 cup flour
1/2 teaspoon cinnamon
4 cups fresh sliced peaches
Prepared pie shell
2 tablespoons butter
Milk
Sugar

Preheat oven to 425.

Combine first four ingredients. Mix well. Place in pie shell and dot with butter. Top with pie crust; cut slits in top. Brush top with milk and sprinkle lightly with sugar. Bake at 425 degrees for 35-45 minutes.

*Tip: If edges brown too fast, cover edges with strips of tin foil.

Grandmother's Special White Cake
with peaches and cream!

1/2 cup shortening
1 cup sugar
2 eggs
1 tablespoon vanilla
2 cups flour
1/2 teaspoon salt
3 teaspoons baking powder
1 cup milk
Whipped cream, sweetened
Fresh ripe peaches
Mint

Preheat oven to 350.

Cream together shortening, sugar and eggs. Stir in vanilla. Sift flour, salt, and baking powder together. Alternately add dry ingredients and milk to shortening mixture. Batter will be thick. Pour into two 9 inch round greased layer pans. Bake at 350 degrees for about 30 minutes. When cooled, fill and top with sweetened whipped cream. Garnish with fresh peaches and mint sprigs.

Peach Cake

1 package (3 ounces) peach Jello
3/4 cup boiling water
4 eggs
2 boxes butter pecan cake mix
3/4 cup canned peaches, pureed
1/2 cup peach juice
2 cups powdered sugar
Fresh peach slices

Preheat oven to 350.

Dissolve Jello in water. Add eggs and beat 2-3 minutes.
Add cake mix and pureed peaches and beat 2 minutes
more. Bake in a greased 9x13 pan at 350 for 40 minutes.
Remove from oven when center is done. While still
hot, prick holes in cake with a fork. Mix peach juice
and powdered sugar together and spread over hot cake.
Garnish with fresh peach slices.

Gingerbread Peach Cake

2 tablespoons butter or margarine
1/4 cup corn syrup
1/4 cup brown sugar
1 can (15 ounces) peach slices, drained
1/2 cup Macadamia nuts

Preheat oven to 350.

Melt butter in 7x11 rectangular cake pan. Pour in syrup and add brown sugar; blend. Arrange peach slices in pan. Sprinkle nuts evenly on top of peaches.

Gingerbread:

1/3 cup butter or shortening
1/2 cup sugar
1 beaten egg
2/3 cup light molasses
2 cups flour
2 teaspoons baking powder
1/4 teaspoon soda
1 teaspoon cinnamon
2 teaspoons ginger
3/4 cup milk

Cream butter (or shortening) and sugar. Add egg; beat thoroughly. Add molasses. Beat. Alternately add sifted dry ingredients and milk. Pour batter over peaches. Bake at 350 for 40 minutes or until done.

Cream Cheese Peach Cake

3/4 cup flour
1 teaspoon baking powder
1 egg
1 package (3 ounces) cook vanilla pudding -- not instant
3 tablespoons butter, softened
1/2 cup milk

1 can (15 ounces) sliced peaches, drain and reserve juice

1 package (8 ounces) cream cheese
1/2 cup sugar
3 tablespoons reserved juice

Preheat oven to 350.

Combine first set of ingredients in mixing bowl. Beat 2 minutes at moderate speed. Pour in greased 9 inch round pan. Top batter with sliced peaches. In separate bowl, cream together cream cheese, sugar, and reserved juice. Spoon cream cheese mixture to within 1 inch of the edge of the batter. Bake at 350 degrees for 30-36 minutes or until crust is golden brown. Filling will appear soft. Store in refrigerator.

Cookies & Cobblers

Individual Peachie Pizzas

Pre made sugar cookie dough
Fresh or canned peaches
Fresh blueberries and or raspberries

Preheat oven according to sugar cookie dough package directions. Prepare enough dough (slice or roll into balls) for 12 cookies. Bake according to package directions. Slice peach into 12 slices.

Topping:

2 tablespoons peach syrup (see recipe page 93) or peach juice
1 teaspoon vanilla extract
2 tablespoons instant vanilla pudding
4 ounces cream cheese, softened
1/2 cup powdered sugar

While cookies are baking, in small bowl stir together peach syrup (or peach juice) and vanilla extract. Add vanilla pudding and stir until smooth. Blend in cream cheese and powdered sugar and whip until smooth.

Topping can be served on hot or cooled cookies. If served hot, top with slice of peach and sprinkle with cinnamon. If served on cooled cookies, chop peach slice into eight sections and place on topping along with blueberries or raspberries.

Peach Dainties

2 cups all-purpose flour
2 teaspoons sugar
1 cup butter
1 package (8 ounces) cream cheese
Peach jam
Brown Sugar
Chopped nuts

Preheat oven to 375.

In large bowl, mix flour and sugar. Cut butter and cream cheese into flour mixture until coarse and crumbly. Knead into a ball; chill 1 hour.

Remove dough from refrigerator. Roll out on ungreased cookie sheet to edges. Bake at 375 for 10-15 minutes or until edges start to brown. Remove from oven. While still warm, spread jam over surface and cut into 1-1/2 inch squares. Sprinkle with brown sugar and nuts.

Peach Coconut Chews

1/2 cup peach syrup (see recipe on page 93)
1 cup powdered sugar
1 teaspoon vanilla
1/4 teaspoon almond extract
1/2 cup pecans
1 cup dried chopped peaches

Stir together syrup and sugar in small saucepan. Bring to a boil, stirring constantly. Boil 1 minute. Remove from heat. Stir in vanilla, almond extract, pecans, and peaches. Drop by spoonfuls onto waxed paper and allow to cool.

Peach Snickerdoodles

1 cup shortening, softened
1-1/2 cup sugar
2 eggs
2-3/4 cups sifted flour
2 teaspoon cream of tartar
1 teaspoon soda
1/4 teaspoon salt
2 tablespoons finely minced dry peaches
2 tablespoons sugar
2 teaspoons cinnamon

Preheat oven to 400.

Cream shortening, sugar, and eggs. Sift dry ingredients together then slowly add to shortening mixture. Roll dough into balls the size of small walnuts. Combine peaches, brown sugar, and cinnamon; rough balls in mixture. Place 2 inches apart on ungreased baking sheet. Bake until lightly browned, but still soft, at 400 degrees for 8-10 minutes.

Esther's Cobbler

1/2 cup flour
1/2 teaspoon baking powder
2 tablespoons soft butter
1/2 cup sugar
1/2 teaspoon salt
1 egg, slightly beaten
Fresh peaches or pie filling

Preheat oven to 350.

Combine first six ingredients and beat until smooth. Set aside. Cover bottom of greased cake pan with sliced peaches or pie filling. Heat in 350 degree oven until peaches are hot. Remove from oven. Drop flour mixture by spoonfuls over hot fruit. Dough will spread as it bakes. Bake at 350 degrees until golden brown.

Caramel Cobbler

1 tablespoon butter
2 cans (29 ounces each) peach slices
1 box (16 ounces) pound cake mix
1 cup Pecan Sandies, crumbed

Preheat oven according to pound cake mix directions.

In 9x13 pan, melt butter. Spread over bottom of pan. Arrange peach slices in butter. Mix pound cake according to package directions and fold in Pecan Sandies. Bake according to pound cake mix directions. Top with caramel sauce.

Caramel sauce:

1/2 cup evaporated milk
1/2 cup butter
1/2 cup brown sugar
1 teaspoon vanilla

Combine all ingredients in small pan and stir over medium heat until sugar is dissolved. Bring to a low boil. Remove from heat and pour over cobbler.

Fast Peach Cobbler

1 can (29 ounces) sliced peaches, reserve syrup
1 box yellow cake mix
1/2 cup melted butter or margarine

Preheat oven to 325.

Place peaches in bottom of greased cake pan. Sprinkle
with cake mix. Pour butter and reserved syrup evenly
over cake mix. Bake at 325 for 1 hour or until done.

Jammin' Spiced Peach Cookies

1 batch Spiced Peach Refrigerator Jam (see recipe on page 116)
Pre made sugar cookie dough

Preheat oven according to cookie package directions.

Roll dough into balls and place on cookie sheet. Depress center of each ball with a spoon, creating a deep hollow, and fill with 1 teaspoon of Spiced Peach Jam. Bake according to directions. Add one to two minutes to baking time if centers seem doughy.

NOTES

Peach skins provide dietary fiber.

Desserts

Tangy Peach Pudding

1 small package (3 ounces) vanilla instant pudding OR
1 small package (3 ounces) vanilla cook and serve pudding
1 batch Spiced Peach Refrigerator Jam (recipe on page 116)

For cold pudding, use instant pudding mix. For hot pudding, use cook and serve mix. Prepare pudding according to package directions. Stir in Spiced Peach Jam. Top with peach slices.

Old Fashioned Peach Pudding

3/4 cup water
3/4 cup brown sugar
2 teaspoons cornstarch
1 cup pureed fresh or canned peaches
1 teaspoon vanilla

In small saucepan, stir water and sugar over medium heat until sugar is dissolved. Whisk in cornstarch and bring to a boil, stirring constantly. Boil gently until thickened. Add peaches and vanilla and simmer 1 minute.

Peaches 'n Chips with Cinnamon Sauce

1 sheet puff pastry dough
Fresh ripe peaches, peeled and sliced
Vanilla ice cream

Preheat oven according to pastry dough package directions.

Lay out pastry dough on cookie sheet. With a pizza cutter, cut into triangles (about the size of a tortilla chip) and separate. Bake according to package directions or until puffed and golden brown. Serve warm with peaches and vanilla ice cream. Top with cinnamon sauce.

Cinnamon Sauce:

1/2 cup honey
1/4 cup peach juice
1 cup powdered sugar
1 cup peach syrup (see recipe on page 93)
1 teaspoon cinnamon

In small pan combine honey, peach juice, and powdered sugar. Stir until sugar is dissolved. Stir in peach syrup and cinnamon and blend well. Serve hot on Peaches 'n Chips.

*Also great on rolls, pancakes, or muffins!

Peach Sorbet

1 cup sugar
1/2 cup water
2 cups pureed fresh or canned peaches
2-4 tablespoons lemon juice

In medium saucepan, bring sugar and water to boil, stirring constantly. Add pureed peaches and boil 1 minute.
Add lemon juice and place mixture in freezer safe container until solid or freeze in ice cube trays (see lemonade and smoothie recipes on pages 13 and 15)

Peach Squares

2 sheets puff pastry dough, thawed
1 package (8 ounces) cream cheese, softened
1 teaspoon vanilla
1/2 cup powdered sugar
1 egg, beaten
Fresh or canned peach slices
1/2 cup cinnamon sauce (see recipe on page 74)
Powdered sugar (optional)

Preheat oven according to pastry dough directions.

Place first pastry sheet into bottom of lightly greased 9x9 pan. Bake according to package directions until just puffed and light golden brown. Remove from oven. Blend together cream cheese, vanilla, powdered sugar, and egg. Spread on top of baked pastry. Top with peach slices and drizzle with 1/4 cup cinnamon sauce. Lay out second pastry sheet on top of peaches. Drizzle with remaining sauce. Bake at 350 for 30-35 minutes or until pastry is golden brown. Cool and cut into squares. If desired, sprinkle with powdered sugar.

Raspberry Peach Supreme

1-1/2 cups butter cookies, crumbed
1/4 cup melted butter

1/2 cup melted butter
1 cup powdered sugar
2 eggs
1/3 cup chopped walnuts
2 cups fresh peaches, sliced
2 cups fresh raspberries
1 cup whipping cream, whipped

Preheat oven to 350.

In food processor, crumb cookies. Mix 1 cup crumbs with 1/4 cup butter and press into bottom of 8 inch square pan. Cream together 1/2 cup butter and sugar. Add eggs one at a time and beat well after each addition. Pour mixture over crumbs. Sprinkle with chopped walnuts. Bake at 350 degrees for 20-30 minutes or until firm in center. Cool. Top with peaches, raspberries, and whipped cream. Sprinkle with remaining crumbs. Chill thoroughly.

Peach Shorties

Fresh ripe peaches
Shortcake cups or sliced pound cake
Whipped Cream

Wash, peel, and pit peaches. Slice peaches and divide between shortcake cups or cake slices. Top with whipped cream.

Easy Melba

Vanilla ice cream
Fresh peach halves
Raspberry jam, warmed

Place one scoop of ice cream in each peach half. Pour
raspberry jam over top.

Peach Tapioca

2-1/4 cups milk
1/2 cup peach juice
1/2 cup sugar
1 egg, beaten
3 tablespoons quick cook tapioca
1 teaspoon vanilla
1/2 cup diced fresh peaches

Mix first five ingredients together in small saucepan and let stand 5 minutes. Over medium heat, stir constantly and bring to a full boil. Remove from heat. Stir in vanilla and peaches; chill.

Harvest Trifle

Spice cake, canned pumpkin, and peaches add a "Wow!" to this yummy trifle

1 spice cake mix
1/3 cup canned pumpkin
1 can (14 ounces) sweetened condensed milk
1 1/3 cup milk
1 package (3 ounces) instant vanilla pudding
1/4 cup canned pumpkin
8-10 slices pound cake
1 jar (18 ounces) peach preserves
1 large carton Cool Whip, partially thawed
3 cups fresh or canned peaches, sliced

Preheat oven according to spice cake mix instructions.

Mix spice cake according to package directions except substitute pumpkin for oil (approximately 1/3 cup). Turn out in 9x13 cake pan and bake according to package directions. Cool cake after baking. Slice into 3/4 inch squares.

Stir together condensed milk and milk. Mix in vanilla pudding then chill for 5 minutes. Blend in pumpkin.

Layer bottom of trifle bowl with pound cake; break or cut into halves to conform to shape of bowl. Spread 1/2 of the preserves on the pound cake. Add layer of Cool Whip. Add 1/2 of the peaches. Add layer of spice cake squares. Top with vanilla pudding mixture. Add second layer of pound cake topped with remainder of preserves and another layer of spice cake squares. Add last of peaches and top with remaining Cool Whip. Chill.

STUFFED FRESH PEACHES WITH SWEET PEACH SAUCE

3/4 cup graham crackers, crumbed
1/4 cup brown sugar
1/4 cup granulated sugar
2 egg yolks, beaten
1/2 teaspoon vanilla
8 fresh ripe peaches, halved
Chopped almonds

Preheat oven to 350.

In small bowl, stir together graham cracker crumbs, sugars, egg yolks, and vanilla. Wash and peel peaches. Remove pits and cut peaches into halves. Use a sharp melon baller to round out centers of peaches. Fill centers with graham cracker mixture and sprinkle generously with chopped almonds. Bake at 350 degrees for 15 minutes. Drizzle peaches with sweet peach sauce.

Sauce:

1 tablespoon mashed ripe peaches
1/4 cup sweetened condensed milk

In small saucepan, combine peaches and condensed milk. Heat until just bubbly.

Cheesecake
with Peach Glaze

Crust:

1 cup sifted flour

1/4 cup sugar

1 teaspoon grated lemon peel

1/2 cup butter

1 egg yolk, slightly beaten

1/2 teaspoon vanilla

Preheat oven to 400.

Combine flour, sugar, and lemon peel. Cut in butter until mixture is crumbly. Add yolk and vanilla; blend. Pat 1/3 of dough into bottom of buttered 9" spring-form pan (sides removed). Bake at 400 degrees for approximately 6 minutes or until golden. Cool. Butter sides of pan and attach to bottom. Pat remaining dough evenly onto sides (about 2 inches high).

Filling:

5 packages (8 ounces each) cream cheese, softened

1/4 teaspoon vanilla

3/4 teaspoon grated lemon peel

1-3/4 cups sugar

3 tablespoons flour

5 eggs

2 egg yolks

1 cup heavy cream

Beat cream cheese until fluffy. Add vanilla and peel. Mix sugar and flour together and gradually blend into cheese. Add eggs and yolks, one at a time. Beat well after each. Gently stir in cream. Turn into crust. Bake at 500 degrees for 5 to 8 minutes or until top edges of crust are golden brown. Reduce heat to 200 degrees; bake 1 additional hour. Remove from oven; cool at least 3 - 4 hours. Remove sides of pan. Top with peach glaze (see recipe on page 121).

Peach Banana Sherbet

1 cup sugar
3 tablespoons lemon juice
3 tablespoons peach juice
1 fresh or canned peach
1 banana
1 cup no fat Half and Half

In small pan, stir and cook sugar and juices over medium low heat until sugar is dissolved. Cool. Meanwhile, puree peach and banana. Stir together Half and Half and pureed fruit with mixture from pan. Pour into container and freeze.

Jello Melba

1 small package (3 ounces) raspberry Jello
1 cup boiling water
2 cups raspberry ice cream
1 can (15 ounces) sliced peaches, drain and reserve juice
1 small package (3 ounces) peach Jello
1 cup boiling water
3/4 cup cold peach juice

Dissolve raspberry Jello in 1 cup boiling water. Add 2 cups raspberry ice cream. Stir until melted and smooth. Chill until set. Arrange peach slices on Jello. In medium bowl, dissolve peach Jello in 1 cup boiling water. Stir in 3/4 cup cold peach juice. Chill until partially set. Pour over top of peaches. Chill until well set then remove from refrigerator and unmold.

Baked Peach/Rice Pudding

1/2 cup rice
1/2 teaspoon salt
4 cups milk
2/3 cup brown sugar
1/4 teaspoon nutmeg
1/2 cup diced canned peaches
1 teaspoon vanilla

Combine rice, salt, milk, and sugar. Pour into greased baking dish and bake at 300 degrees for 1 hour, stirring several times. Add nutmeg, peaches, and vanilla; continue baking 2 to 2-1/2 hours.

Peach Bars

2 eggs
1-1/2 cup sugar
2-1/4 cups flour
1-1/2 teaspoon soda
1 teaspoon vanilla
1 can (15 ounces) peaches, drained, cut into small pieces
1 cup shredded coconut
1/2 cup chopped almonds

Preheat oven to 350.

Cream together eggs and sugar. Mix in flour, soda, and vanilla. Fold in peaches. Spread into 9x13 greased pan and sprinkle with coconut and almonds. Bake at 350 degrees for 30-40 minutes or until center is done. Top with drizzle.

Drizzle:

3/4 cup powdered sugar
1/4 cup evaporated milk
1 tablespoon sour cream

Combine ingredients in small saucepan. Bring to boil and boil 2 minutes while stirring constantly.

Peach Bread Pudding

1-1/2 cups milk
2 eggs, slightly beaten
4 slices toast, cubed
1 cup fresh or canned diced peaches
1 cup sugar

Preheat oven to 350.

Scald milk. Add eggs and mix well. Add other ingredients, stir, and pour into buttered 1-1/2 quart casserole. Bake at 350 degrees for one hour or until custard sets.

Quick Peach Ice Cream

Pasteurized egg substitute equal to five eggs
1-3/4 cup sugar
1 can evaporated milk
1 can sweetened condensed milk
2 tablespoons vanilla
Dash salt
1 can (15 ounces) diced peaches, drained

Combine all ingredients; blend well. Put into ice cream freezer and add milk to within 2 inches of top. Follow directions with freezer to freeze ice cream.

Supreme Peach Ice Cream

3-1/2 cups sugar
1/2 cup + 1 tablespoon lemon juice
Juice from one orange or 1 tablespoon frozen concentrate
3 cups whipping cream
2 cans (13 ounces each) evaporated milk
1 teaspoon vanilla
1 teaspoon almond flavor
3 cups peaches, mash with potato masher
1/2 cup crushed pineapple (optional)

Mix all ingredients together and add enough milk to fill
a 4-quart ice cream maker to 3/4 full.

Breakfasts

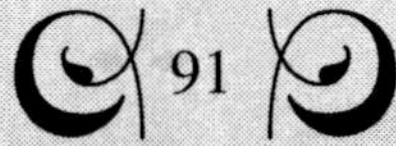

Peach Fritters

1 1/2 cup chopped fresh or canned peaches
1/2 teaspoon lemon juice
1 egg, beaten
1 cup Bisquick
1/2 cup non-fat Half and Half

Combine all ingredients. Mix well. If necessary, thicken batter with flour. Fry in hot oil until golden brown. Serve warm, sprinkled with powdered sugar.

Whole Wheat Waffles with Peach Syrup

5 egg yolks
2 cups -- less 2 tablespoons milk
1/2 cup oil
1-1/2 teaspoon sugar
3 cups whole wheat flour
3 teaspoons baking powder
1/2 teaspoon salt
5 egg whites, beaten

Beat together the first four ingredients. Sift flour, baking powder, and salt. Add to egg yolk mixture and beat until smooth. Fold in egg whites and stir well.

Peach Syrup:

1-1/2 cups sugar
1/2 cup water
3 cups pureed fresh or canned peaches
1 tablespoon lemon

Combine sugar and water in medium saucepan. Stirring constantly, bring to boil over medium heat. Boil 1 minute. Add peach puree. Return to low boil and boil for 5 minutes. Remove from heat. Add lemon juice. Store in refrigerator in tightly sealed container.

Fruity Hash Browns

1 fresh peach, chopped (remove skin)
1/2 red apple, grated with skin on
3 medium par-cooked red potatoes, grated with skins on
2 tablespoons fresh chives
1 tablespoon melted butter
Salt and pepper to taste
1 tablespoon olive oil

In medium bowl, combine peach, apple, potatoes, chives, and butter. Add olive oil to medium skillet. Add potato mixture and fry to a golden brown.

Hearty Peach Flapjacks

2 cups flour
1/2 cup brown sugar
1 teaspoon salt
3 teaspoons baking powder
1 teaspoon cinnamon
2 eggs, separated
1-3/4 cup milk
4 tablespoons butter
1 cup quick oats
1/2 cup minced dried peaches

Sift together flour, sugar, salt, baking powder, and cinnamon. Beat egg yolks and add milk; beat. Slowly add flour mixture to egg mixture, beating slowly until smooth. Add melted butter and fold in egg whites which have been beaten until stiff. Stir in oats and peaches. If batter seems too thick, add a little milk.

Oatmeal Mix

7 cups quick oats
1/2 cup firmly packed brown sugar
1 tablespoon cinnamon
1-1/2 teaspoon nutmeg
1 cup slivered almonds
1 cup minced dried peaches

Combine all ingredients and mix well. Store in a tightly covered container in cool, dry place. When ready to eat, bring 1 cup water to boil and stir in 1 cup mix. Simmer over medium heat for 2-3 minutes.

Breakfast Cobbler

1 cup pancake mix
1 cup peach juice
1 can (15 ounces) sliced peaches
1 package (8 ounces) precooked sausage links, halved
Peach syrup (see recipe on page 93)

Preheat oven to 350 degrees.

Stir together pancake mix and peach juice. Pour into well greased 8x8 cake pan. Arrange peaches and links on top of batter. Bake 30 minutes at 350 degrees. Top with peach syrup.

Peach Granola

1 cup dried peaches, chopped
4 cups rolled oats
1 cup wheat germ
1 cup shredded coconut
1/2 cup sunflower seeds
1/2 cup slivered almonds
1/2 cup brown sugar
3/4 cup honey
1 cup vegetable oil

Combine dry ingredients in a large bowl. In small saucepan, mix brown sugar, honey, and oil together and stir until sugar is dissolved. Pour over dry mixture and mix well. Spread onto two greased cookie sheets. Bake at 300 degrees until lightly browned, 15-20 minutes. Stir every five minutes during baking. Remove from oven to cool. Continue to stir every few minutes. When cooled, store in airtight container.

Peach Crepes

10 pre made crepes
1 package (8 ounces) cream cheese, softened
3/4 cup whipping cream
1 cup peach preserves or peach jam
1/2 cup granulated sugar
2 teaspoons vanilla
1 tablespoon lemon juice
Fresh peaches, sliced
Powdered sugar

Preheat oven to 325.

Beat together cream cheese, whipping cream, preserves (or jam) and sugar until smooth and creamy. Add vanilla and lemon juice and beat again until well blended. Spread 4 tablespoons of the cream cheese mixture over the surface of each crepe. Place peach slices down center of crepes and roll up. Place crepes in greased 13x9 pan and bake 8-10 minutes at 325 degrees. Garnish with additional peaches, or peach topping (below), and powdered sugar.

Peach topping:

1/3 cup whipping cream
1/8 cup Lighthouse peach dessert glaze

Beat whipping cream and glaze until smooth and thick.

Susan's Hot Peach Breakfast

Sliced bananas
Brown sugar to taste
Fresh peach slices
Peach juice

In single serve microwaveable baking dish, layer banana, brown sugar, and peach slices. Pour juice over all and microwave on high 30 seconds or until bubbly.

Sausage Peach Scramble

A great way to use leftover sausage or peaches!

2 cooked sausage patties, or 4 links
6 eggs, beaten
1/4 cup Maple syrup
1 canned peach, chopped
3 tablespoons cream cheese, softened
Cream cheese
4 bagels, sliced

Crumble sausage into medium microwave safe bowl. Stir in eggs, syrup, chopped peach, and cream cheese. Microwave on high. Check every one to two minutes and re stir mixture. Cook approximately 8-10 minutes or until completely cooked through. Spread cream cheese on bagel and add a scoop of eggs for a delectable breakfast sandwich.

Peach Roll-ups

1 package (4 ounces) crescent roll dough
3 tablespoons peach jam or preserves
Cinnamon
Brown sugar

Preheat oven according to crescent roll package directions.

Prepare dough according to package directions topping each triangle with jam or preserves. Sprinkle with cinnamon and roll up. Sprinkle with brown sugar. Bake according to package directions.

Peachy Keen French Toast

1 small package (3 ounces) vanilla instant pudding
1 cup finely chopped fresh or canned peaches
1/8 teaspoon nutmeg
1/8 teaspoon cinnamon
5 eggs, beaten
12 slices wheat or whole grain bread

Prepare pudding according to package directions. Fold in chopped peaches, nutmeg, and cinnamon. Add eggs and mix well. Dip bread slices into mixture. Cook on well greased skillet over medium heat, turning frequently so toast doesn't scorch. Top with maple syrup, cinnamon, and powdered sugar.

Grandma's Peach Cinnamon Rolls

1 yeast cake
1 tablespoon sugar
1 cup warm water
1 cup scalded milk, cooled
3 cups flour
6 tablespoons shortening
1/2 cup sugar
3 eggs, beaten until light

4 cups sifted flour
1/2 teaspoon salt
Melted butter
Brown sugar
Nuts
Cinnamon
1/2 cup dried peaches

Preheat oven to 375.

Dissolve yeast and sugar in warm water. Add scalded milk. Add 3 cups flour and stir until smooth. Cream shortening and sugar. Add to flour mixture. Add eggs then add remainder of flour and salt to make a moderately soft dough. Turn onto floured board and knead lightly. Place in a greased bowl; cover and set aside in a warm place to rise (about 2 hours). Roll out in an oblong shape to 1/4 inch thick. Brush with melted butter and sprinkle with brown sugar, nuts, and cinnamon. Place dried peaches in food processor and process until they resemble cookie crumbs. Sprinkle peaches over dough. Roll dough up then cut and lay rolls side by side in pan. Let rise one hour or until light. Bake 25 minutes at 375 degrees.

This 'n That

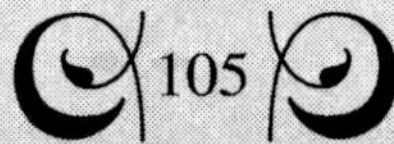

Sweet Fruit Salsa

2 green apples, cut into small pieces
2 cups chopped fresh strawberries
2 cups peeled and chopped fresh peaches
1 cup peeled and chopped kiwi
1/3 cup honey
3 tablespoons peach preserves
1 tablespoon brown sugar

Prepare fruit. Combine honey, preserves, and brown sugar and mix well. Toss mixture with fruit, chill, and serve cold.

Peach Salsa

1 cup chopped fresh ripe peaches
3/4 cup chopped fresh tomatoes
1/2 cup sweet red onion, chopped
1 teaspoon minced garlic
1 green onion, thinly sliced
2 teaspoons cilantro
1 tablespoon olive oil
2 tablespoons lime juice
1 to 2 teaspoons granulated sugar

Combine peaches, tomatoes, red onion, garlic, green onion, and cilantro. Set aside. In separate bowl, whisk olive oil, lime juice, and sugar until sugar is dissolved. Pour over peach mixture and stir gently to combine. Chill. Store in sealed container in refrigerator.

*Great on tortilla chips or try with eggs, fish, or chicken!

Cranberry Peach Relish

1 cup fresh cranberries
1 cup canned mandarin orange slices, drained
2 apples, peeled and diced
2 fresh peaches, peeled and diced
Honey to taste

Wash and prepare fruit. Combine cranberries, oranges, apples, and peaches. Drizzle with honey. Serve with chicken or other meats.

Peach Popsicles

1 teaspoon peach gelatin
1/2 cup milk
1 carton (8 ounces) peach flavored yogurt
1/2 cup fresh or canned peaches, mashed
Popsicle molds

Combine gelatin and milk in saucepan. Heat over low heat until gelatin dissolves. Remove from heat and cool slightly. Stir in yogurt and mashed peaches; blend well. Pour into molds. Freeze until hard (3-4 hours).

Peach Leather

2 cups peaches, pureed
1/2 cup honey
1 teaspoon vanilla
2 teaspoons orange juice concentrate or lemon juice
1 teaspoon cinnamon

Puree peaches in blender. Add honey, vanilla, juice, and cinnamon. Spread evenly on freezer paper to 1/8 inch thickness. Dry in dehydrator at 120 degrees for 6-12 hours, or in the sun for 16-24 hours. Near end of drying time, remove leather from freezer paper and place directly on rack or screen. Leather is done when surface is no longer sticky. Wrap warm leather jelly roll style in plastic wrap. Store in airtight container.

Peach Spread

1 stick (4 ounces) butter
1/2 cup peach pie filling
1/3 cup whipped cream

Combine all ingredients and mix well. Refrigerate in tightly covered container. Great on warm rolls or bread!

Peach Jam

3 cups chopped peaches
3 cups water
1/2 cup lemon juice
1 package (3 ounces) orange Kool-Aid
1 package (2 ounces) pectin
8-1/2 cups sugar

Mash peaches well or puree. Mix peaches, water,
lemon juice, Kool-Aid, and pectin in a large pan.
Bring to a rolling boil. Add sugar. Bring to rolling boil
again. Cook 8 minutes, stirring constantly. Place in
jars and seal.

Peach Facial Scrub

The alpha hydroxy acids in peaches have been used for years in many beauty products to exfoliate, soften wrinkles, and diminish skin spots and blemishes!

1 tablespoon honey
2 tablespoons fresh ripe peach, pureed
1 tablespoon granulated sugar
1 tablespoon oatmeal

Combine all ingredients. Spread mixture on face and massage with fingertips using light, circular motions. Rinse with cool water.

Peach Face Mask

1 fresh ripe peach
1 egg white

Puree peach in blender or food processor. In small bowl, beat egg white just until stiff. Fold peach puree into egg white. With fingertips, apply layer of mask mixture to face and neck. Allow to dry for 20 minutes. Rinse with lukewarm water.

Sour Cream Topping

1/4 cup sour cream
2 teaspoons powdered sugar
1/8 teaspoon cinnamon
Dash of nutmeg
1 fresh ripe peach, diced

Combine sour cream, powdered sugar, cinnamon, and nutmeg. Stir until smooth. Add peach. Makes an excellent topping for waffles!

Variation:

1/2 cup sour cream
1 tablespoon brown sugar
1/8 teaspoon ground cinnamon
1/4 cup pureed peaches

Combine all ingredients and stir until smooth. Serve over fresh peaches or on waffles or pancakes with sliced peaches.

Can't Get Enough Peach Popcorn Bake

7 cups popped popcorn
5 tablespoons butter
3 tablespoons light corn syrup
3/4 cup granulated sugar
1/4 cup Lighthouse peach flavored dessert glaze
1/4 teaspoon baking soda
1 teaspoon vanilla
1 cup finely chopped dried peaches
1 cup cherry flavored Craisins
1 cup pecan pieces

Preheat oven to 300 degrees.

In a small saucepan, combine butter, corn syrup, and sugar. Stir constantly over medium heat until mixture comes to a boil. Boil and stir 1 minute. Reduce heat. Stir in glaze. Cook and stir 5 more minutes. Remove from heat. Stir in soda and vanilla. Place popcorn in large baking dish and stir in peaches, Craisins, and pecans. Pour liquid mixture over popcorn and stir to coat well. Bake at 300 degrees for 10 minutes. Remove from oven and stir. Return to oven and bake an additional 5-10 minutes. Remove and place in bowl to cool.

SMALL BATCH
Spiced Peach
Refrigerator Jam

1 fresh or canned peach
1/8 to 1/4 cup firmly packed brown sugar (to taste)
1/4 teaspoon nutmeg
1/8 teaspoon ground cloves
1/8 teaspoon ground cinnamon
2 tablespoons peach Jello
1/4 cup sliced almonds

For chunky textured jam, mash peach with a potato masher. For finer texture, puree in blender or food processor. Add mashed or pureed peach to small pan. Over medium heat, stir in brown sugar, nutmeg, cloves, cinnamon, and peach Jello. Bring to a boil, stirring constantly. Remove from heat and add almonds.

*Can be used hot or cold on pancakes, waffles, biscuits, or ice cream. Store remainder in refrigerator.

Peach Honey Butter

1 stick (4 ounces) butter, melted
1/3 cup honey
1 fresh or canned peach, pureed

In small bowl, combine butter, honey, and peach puree. Whip. Chill until thickened. Keep refrigerated in a tightly sealed container for 3-4 days.

*Great on muffins!

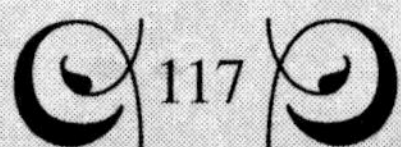

Peachy Angel Frosting

1 package (3 ounces) peach Jello
1/2 cup boiling water
2 cups sugar
1 cup water
1/4 teaspoon Cream of Tarter
4 egg whites

Dissolve Jello in boiling water. In small saucepan, cook together sugar, water, and Cream of Tarter until syrup spins a thread an inch long. Beat egg whites until stiff. Pour hot sugar mixture into egg whites while beating constantly. When well blended, add Jello mixture (which has cooled but not set) and beat well. Cool before putting on cake.

Tropical Ham Sauce

1 can (13 ounces) pineapple chunks, drain and reserve juice
1 can (15.4 ounces) diced peaches, drain and reserve juice
1/3 cup brown sugar
4 teaspoons flour
1/8 teaspoon salt
1 teaspoon dry mustard
Maraschino cherries, halved (optional)

In medium saucepan, combine syrup from pineapple and peaches. Juice from both cans of fruit should equal 1/2 cup each; if short, add water. Stir in brown sugar until dissolved. Whisk in flour, salt, and dry mustard and blend until smooth. Bring to boil, stirring constantly, until thickened. Reduce heat to low. Add pineapple chunks and peaches. Pour sauce over ham slices. If desired, serve with Maraschino cherry halves.

Peach Honey Frosting

1/4 cup peach jam
1 tablespoon honey
1/3 cup powdered sugar

Combine ingredients and mix until smooth.

Peach Glaze

2 to 3 cups fresh ripe peaches
1 cup water
1-1/2 tablespoons cornstarch
1/2 to 3/4 cup sugar to taste

Puree peaches; add water and cook over medium heat for 2 minutes. Mix cornstarch with sugar and stir into peach mixture. Bring to a boil, stirring constantly. Cook and stir until thick and clear.

Popcorn Balls

1/3 cup butter
1 package (10.5 ounces) miniature marshmallows
1 small package (3 ounces) peach Jello
12 cups popped popcorn
Butter or margarine

In large microwave safe bowl, microwave butter and marshmallows on high for approximately 2 minutes. Stir in Jello. Mix well. Pour mixture over popcorn and coat well. Coat hands with butter or margarine and form popcorn mixture into balls.

Nature's Best

We saved the best for last!

1 fresh ripe peach

If you're lucky enough to live in an area where peaches are grown, enjoy eating a ripe peach right from the tree! Or, slice and place in a bowl. Pour on a little milk or cream and sprinkle with sugar. Enjoy!

Notes

The ancient Chinese first cultivated peaches as early as 1000 BC where they were considered to be a symbol of longevity.

NOTES

In China, the peach is thought to have mystical attributes. It supposedly brings, abundance, luck, and protection.

About the Author

Lori Nawyn designed the popular children's book, *Sarah Jane's Very Best Story Ever*, and completed the artwork and design for acclaimed musician C.S. Bezas' CD, *A Time for Ana*.

An aspiring author, her award winning short stories are included in three books, *The Magic and the Miracle of Christmas, Volumes I* and *II*, and *Hearts and Hands: Stories of Hope for Mothers*. She is currently working on writing and illustrating a children's book of her own, *The Keepers of the Star. Peach 101: Recipes Your Mother Never Told You About* is her first cookbook. Her second cookbook, *Recipes from the Heart*, is due out in 2007.

Visit Lori at her website, **www.lorinawyn.com**.

Additional copies available at bookstores
or directly from

**Brigham Distributing
110 South 800 West
Brigham City, Utah 84302**

Office 1.435.723.6611
Fax 1.435.723.6644

www.brighamdistributing.com

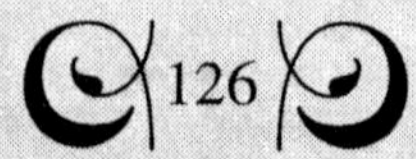